MAD LIBS®

GOBBLE GOBBLE MAD LIBS

W9-DCO-742

concept created by Roger Price & Leonard Stern

Mad Libs
An Imprint of Penguin Random House

MAD LIBS
Penguin Young Readers Group
An Imprint of Penguin Random House LLC

Mad Libs format and text copyright © 2013 by Penguin Random House LLC.
All rights reserved.

Concept created by Roger Price & Leonard Stern

Published by Mad Libs,
an imprint of Penguin Random House LLC,
345 Hudson Street, New York, New York 10014.
Printed in the USA.

ISBN 9780843172928
10

MAD LIBS is a registered trademark of Penguin Random House LLC.

MAD LIBS® is a game for people who don't like games! It can be played by one, two, three, four, or forty.

• RIDICULOUSLY SIMPLE DIRECTIONS

In this tablet you will find stories containing blank spaces where words are left out. One player, the READER, selects one of these stories. The READER does not tell anyone what the story is about. Instead, he/she asks the other players, the WRITERS, to give him/her words. These words are used to fill in the blank spaces in the story.

• TO PLAY

The READER asks each WRITER in turn to call out a word—an adjective or a noun or whatever the space calls for—and uses them to fill in the blank spaces in the story. The result is a MAD LIBS® game.

When the READER then reads the completed MAD LIBS® game to the other players, they will discover that they have written a story that is fantastic, screamingly funny, shocking, silly, crazy, or just plain dumb—depending upon which words each WRITER called out.

• EXAMPLE (*Before* and *After*)

" _____ !" he said _____
    EXCLAMATION   ADVERB

as he jumped into his convertible _____ and
                                NOUN

drove off with his _____ wife.
              ADJECTIVE

" *Ouch* !" he said *stupidly*
    EXCLAMATION   ADVERB

as he jumped into his convertible *cat* and
                                NOUN

drove off with his *brave* wife.
              ADJECTIVE

In case you have forgotten what adjectives, adverbs, nouns, and verbs are, here is a quick review:

An ADJECTIVE describes something or somebody. *Lumpy, soft, ugly, messy,* and *short* are adjectives.

An ADVERB tells how something is done. It modifies a verb and usually ends in "ly." *Modestly, stupidly, greedily,* and *carefully* are adverbs.

A NOUN is the name of a person, place, or thing. *Sidewalk, umbrella, bridle, bathtub,* and *nose* are nouns.

A VERB is an action word. *Run, pitch, jump,* and *swim* are verbs. Put the verbs in past tense if the directions say PAST TENSE. *Ran, pitched, jumped,* and *swam* are verbs in the past tense.

When we ask for A PLACE, we mean any sort of place: a country or city (*Spain, Cleveland*) or a room (*bathroom, kitchen*).

An EXCLAMATION or SILLY WORD is any sort of funny sound, gasp, grunt, or outcry, like *Wow!, Ouch!, Whomp!, Ick!,* and *Gadzooks!*

When we ask for specific words, like a NUMBER, a COLOR, an ANIMAL, or a PART OF THE BODY, we mean a word that is one of those things, like *seven, blue, horse,* or *head.*

When we ask for a PLURAL, it means more than one. For example, *cat* pluralized is *cats.*

MAD LIBS® is fun to play with friends, but you can also play it by yourself! To begin with, DO NOT look at the story on the page below. Fill in the blanks on this page with the words called for. Then, using the words you have selected, fill in the blank spaces in the story.

Now you've created your own hilarious MAD LIBS® game!

WHAT I'M THANKFUL FOR

ADJECTIVE _____

PERSON IN ROOM _____

NOUN _____

NOUN _____

NOUN _____

PART OF THE BODY _____

PLURAL NOUN _____

TYPE OF LIQUID _____

PART OF THE BODY _____

NOUN _____

ADJECTIVE _____

NOUN _____

NOUN _____

PLURAL NOUN _____

NUMBER _____

NOUN _____

MAD LIBS®

WHAT I'M THANKFUL FOR

This Thanksgiving, I'm thankful for all the _____ things in
ADJECTIVE

my life. Even though I complain about how _____ is
PERSON IN ROOM

always getting on my nerves, or how my _____ homework
NOUN

is boring, or how I hate cleaning my _____, I know I am
NOUN

a very lucky _____. I have a roof over my _____.
NOUN   PART OF THE BODY

I always have enough _____ to eat and _____
PLURAL NOUN   TYPE OF LIQUID

to drink. I have a good _____ on my shoulders, and I am
PART OF THE BODY

as healthy as a/an _____. My _____ family loves
NOUN   ADJECTIVE

me, even when I act like a devil-_____. And my friends
NOUN

always have my best _____ at heart. Yep, I've got all the
NOUN

_____ I need, and now I get to eat a/an _____-course
PLURAL NOUN   NUMBER

Thanksgiving meal, too. What more could a/an _____
NOUN

ask for?

MAD LIBS® is fun to play with friends, but you can also play it by yourself! To begin with, DO NOT look at the story on the page below. Fill in the blanks on this page with the words called for. Then, using the words you have selected, fill in the blank spaces in the story.

Now you've created your own hilarious MAD LIBS® game!

WHAT'S FOR DINNER?

NOUN _____

PERSON IN ROOM _____

VERB _____

PART OF THE BODY (PLURAL) _____

ADJECTIVE _____

NOUN _____

NOUN _____

PLURAL NOUN _____

TYPE OF LIQUID _____

ADJECTIVE _____

NOUN _____

NOUN _____

NOUN _____

PLURAL NOUN _____

PERSON IN ROOM (FEMALE) _____

NOUN _____

PART OF THE BODY (PLURAL) _____

It was Thanksgiving, and the scent of succulent roast _____
                                                          NOUN

wafted through my house. "_____, it's time to
                          PERSON IN ROOM

_____!" my mother called. I couldn't wait to get my
        VERB

_____ on that _____ Thanksgiving meal.
PART OF THE BODY (PLURAL)   ADJECTIVE

My family sat around the dining-room _____. The table
                                              NOUN

was laid out with every kind of _____ imaginable. There was
                                        NOUN

a basket of hot buttered _____ and glasses of sparkling
                              PLURAL NOUN

_____. The _____ turkey sat, steaming,
  TYPE OF LIQUID   ADJECTIVE

next to a tureen of _____ gravy. A bowl of ruby-red
                          NOUN

_____ sauce, a sweet-_____ casserole, and a dish of
     NOUN   NOUN

mashed _____ tempted my taste buds. But the dish I
         PLURAL NOUN

looked forward to most was Grandma _____'s
                                      PERSON IN ROOM (FEMALE)

famous _____ pie. Thanksgiving is my favorite holiday,
          NOUN

_____ down.
PART OF THE BODY (PLURAL)

MAD LIBS® is fun to play with friends, but you can also play it by yourself! To begin with, DO NOT look at the story on the page below. Fill in the blanks on this page with the words called for. Then, using the words you have selected, fill in the blank spaces in the story.

Now you've created your own hilarious MAD LIBS® game!

BALLOON GOES BUST

ADJECTIVE _____

A PLACE _____

NOUN _____

A PLACE _____

VERB ENDING IN "ING" _____

ADJECTIVE _____

EXCLAMATION _____

NOUN _____

PART OF THE BODY _____

ADJECTIVE _____

PART OF THE BODY (PLURAL) _____

PART OF THE BODY _____

PLURAL NOUN _____

PART OF THE BODY (PLURAL) _____

VERB ENDING IN "ING" _____

MAD LIBS

BALLOON GOES BUST

This story is to be read aloud by two _____ narrators.
ADJECTIVE

TV Announcer #1: Welcome, viewers, to the thirty-third annual

_____ Thanksgiving parade.
A PLACE

TV Announcer #2: These floats are a/an _____
NOUN

to behold. Look! The famous _____ turkey balloon
A PLACE

is _____ our way!
VERB ENDING IN "ING"

TV Anouncer #1: Oh no! The balloon is caught on a/an

_____ traffic light!
ADJECTIVE

TV Announcer #2: _____! It appears a/an
EXCLAMATION

_____ has pierced the balloon's _____!
NOUN   PART OF THE BODY

The turkey is losing air at a/an _____ rate!
ADJECTIVE

TV Announcer #1: Children along the parade route are crying their

_____ out. This is not a sight for the faint
PART OF THE BODY (PLURAL)

of _____, folks.
PART OF THE BODY

TV Announcer #2: TV viewers, if you have small

_____ at home, cover their _____!
PLURAL NOUN   PART OF THE BODY (PLURAL)

It's a Thanks-_____ disaster!
VERB ENDING IN "ING"

MAD LIBS® is fun to play with friends, but you can also play it by yourself! To begin with, DO NOT look at the story on the page below. Fill in the blanks on this page with the words called for. Then, using the words you have selected, fill in the blank spaces in the story.

Now you've created your own hilarious MAD LIBS® game!

HOW TO ROAST A TURKEY

PART OF THE BODY _____

NUMBER _____

TYPE OF LIQUID _____

PLURAL NOUN _____

PLURAL NOUN _____

PLURAL NOUN _____

NOUN _____

NOUN _____

ADVERB _____

PART OF THE BODY _____

NOUN _____

TYPE OF LIQUID _____

PART OF THE BODY _____

PART OF THE BODY _____

NUMBER _____

ADJECTIVE _____

ADVERB _____

MAD LIBS
HOW TO ROAST A TURKEY

To roast a turkey, you first have to remove the turkey's neck, heart,

gizzard, and _____. Then preheat the oven to _____
        PART OF THE BODY   NUMBER

degrees. Wash out the turkey with _____, then fill it with
                                      TYPE OF LIQUID

stuffing. Popular stuffing ingredients include cubed _____,
                                     PLURAL NOUN

celery, raisins, onion, and _____. Close up the turkey
                         PLURAL NOUN

cavity using string or metal _____. Rub melted
                          PLURAL NOUN

_____ or _____ oil all over the outside of the turkey,
   NOUN   NOUN

then sprinkle it _____ with salt and pepper. Place the whole
                ADVERB

thing, _____ down, in a pan, and add several sprigs of fresh
      PART OF THE BODY

_____. Put it in the oven with a tray beneath it to catch any
   NOUN

_____ that might drip from the turkey's _____.
TYPE OF LIQUID   PART OF THE BODY

Every half hour, stick a thermometer into the turkey's _____
                                        PART OF THE BODY

to make sure it doesn't rise above _____ degrees. The turkey
                             NUMBER

is done when its juices appear _____. Take the turkey out of the
                          ADJECTIVE

oven, carve _____, and enjoy!
        ADVERB

MAD LIBS® is fun to play with friends, but you can also play it by yourself! To begin with, DO NOT look at the story on the page below. Fill in the blanks on this page with the words called for. Then, using the words you have selected, fill in the blank spaces in the story.

Now you've created your own hilarious MAD LIBS® game!

FOOTBALL FIASCO

PLURAL NOUN _____

A PLACE _____

PLURAL NOUN _____

NUMBER _____

SAME NUMBER _____

NOUN _____

ADJECTIVE _____

ADVERB _____

NUMBER _____

VERB (PAST TENSE) _____

ADJECTIVE _____

ADJECTIVE _____

VERB ENDING IN "ING" _____

PART OF THE BODY _____

ADVERB _____

VERB (PAST TENSE) _____

ADVERB _____

MAD LIBS

FOOTBALL FIASCO

It was the fourth quarter in the big Thanksgiving Day matchup

between the Detroit _____ and (the) _____
    _____PLURAL NOUN   A PLACE

_____. The score was tied _____–_____,
    PLURAL NOUN   NUMBER   SAME NUMBER

and you could feel the tension throughout _____ Stadium.
                                                      NOUN

With five minutes left in the game, Detroit had just called a time-out

when, suddenly, fans noticed a/an _____ commotion down
                                            ADJECTIVE

on the field. A turkey had somehow gotten loose and was running

_____ across the _____-yard line! The crowd
    ADVERB   NUMBER

_____ with laughter as the referees chased the
    VERB (PAST TENSE)

_____ bird. Members of both teams joined the refs in chasing
    ADJECTIVE

the _____ turkey, which tried to outrun the Detroit
          ADJECTIVE

_____ back who eventually caught him by the
    VERB ENDING IN "ING"

_____. After that, the tension throughout the stadium
    PART OF THE BODY

_____ broken, the fans hardly cared who won or
    ADVERB

_____. The runaway turkey had _____ stolen
    VERB (PAST TENSE)   ADVERB

the show!

MAD LIBS® is fun to play with friends, but you can also play it by yourself! To begin with, DO NOT look at the story on the page below. Fill in the blanks on this page with the words called for. Then, using the words you have selected, fill in the blank spaces in the story.

Now you've created your own hilarious MAD LIBS® game!

THE FIRST THANKSGIVING

NUMBER _____

A PLACE _____

NOUN _____

ADJECTIVE _____

PLURAL NOUN _____

ADJECTIVE _____

PERSON IN ROOM _____

PLURAL NOUN _____

PLURAL NOUN _____

ADJECTIVE _____

ADJECTIVE _____

NUMBER _____

PLURAL NOUN _____

ADJECTIVE _____

NOUN _____

ADVERB _____

PLURAL NOUN _____

ADJECTIVE _____

In late 1620, _____ Pilgrims arrived at Plymouth Rock.
                    NUMBER

They had come all the way from (the) _____ to find religious
                                      A PLACE

freedom in America. But life in the New _____ was not easy.
                                          NOUN

Their first winter was _____, and many _____ fell ill.
                        ADJECTIVE   PLURAL NOUN

Luckily, the following year, a/an _____ Native American
                                   ADJECTIVE

named _____ taught the Pilgrims how to grow crops like
       PERSON IN ROOM

corn and _____. By that November, the Pilgrims had
          PLURAL NOUN

plenty of _____ to harvest, so they decided to have a/an
           PLURAL NOUN

_____ feast. They invited their _____ Native
 ADJECTIVE   ADJECTIVE

American friends to join them, and the festival lasted for _____
                                                            NUMBER

days. They ate the _____ of their harvest as well as deer
                    PLURAL NOUN

and several _____ birds. It was a/an _____
             ADJECTIVE   NOUN

to remember, and has since become known as the first Thanksgiving.

While the menu has changed _____ over the years,
                            ADVERB

Thanksgiving is still a time to celebrate our _____ and our
                                               PLURAL NOUN

_____ fortune.
 ADJECTIVE

MAD LIBS® is fun to play with friends, but you can also play it by yourself! To begin with, DO NOT look at the story on the page below. Fill in the blanks on this page with the words called for. Then, using the words you have selected, fill in the blank spaces in the story.

Now you've created your own hilarious MAD LIBS® game!

TRAVEL DISASTER

ADJECTIVE _____

ADJECTIVE _____

A PLACE _____

PERSON IN ROOM (FEMALE) _____

PERSON IN ROOM (MALE) _____

NOUN _____

NOUN _____

VERB (PAST TENSE) _____

NUMBER _____

NOUN _____

NOUN _____

ADJECTIVE _____

ADJECTIVE _____

ADJECTIVE _____

ADVERB _____

PLURAL NOUN _____

NOUN _____

MAD LIBS®
TRAVEL DISASTER

Flying for Thanksgiving is always a/an _____ nightmare, but

ADJECTIVE

this year was particularly _____. My family was supposed

ADJECTIVE

to go to (the) boring old _____ to visit my aunt

A PLACE

_____ and uncle _____. But when

PERSON IN ROOM (FEMALE)   PERSON IN ROOM (MALE)

we got to the airport, a/an _____ storm delayed our flight.

NOUN

After we boarded the _____, we _____ on the

NOUN   VERB (PAST TENSE)

runway for _____ hours because of a mechanical difficulty.

NUMBER

They eventually drove us back to the gate and rescheduled us on a

new _____. When we finally took off, the pilot said, "Welcome

NOUN

aboard _____ Airlines. Enjoy your _____ flight

NOUN   ADJECTIVE

to Hawaii." *Hawaii?!* We were on the wrong plane! But we embraced

the _____ screwup. Hawaii was a far more _____

ADJECTIVE   ADJECTIVE

destination than our aunt and uncle's! We laughed _____

ADVERB

the whole flight there and enjoyed frozen coconut _____

PLURAL NOUN

on the beach for our Thanksgiving dinner. It was a/an _____

NOUN

to remember!

MAD LIBS® is fun to play with friends, but you can also play it by yourself! To begin with, DO NOT look at the story on the page below. Fill in the blanks on this page with the words called for. Then, using the words you have selected, fill in the blank spaces in the story.

Now you've created your own hilarious MAD LIBS® game!

HOW THANKSGIVING BECAME A HOLIDAY

ADJECTIVE _____

PLURAL NOUN _____

ADJECTIVE _____

A PLACE _____

VERB _____

ADJECTIVE _____

PLURAL NOUN _____

PLURAL NOUN _____

ADJECTIVE _____

ADJECTIVE _____

PERSON IN ROOM _____

ADJECTIVE _____

PLURAL NOUN _____

MAD LIBS®
HOW THANKSGIVING BECAME A HOLIDAY

Even though the first Thanksgiving took place in 1621, Thanksgiving

didn't become a national holiday until a/an _____ woman
ADJECTIVE

named Sarah Josepha Hale came along. In the 1800s, Ms. Hale was

one of the first female _____ at a/an _____
PLURAL NOUN   ADJECTIVE

magazine. She was famous throughout (the) _____ for her
A PLACE

articles encouraging women to _____, exercise, and get a/an
VERB

_____ education. But one of Sarah's biggest ideas was to make
ADJECTIVE

Thanksgiving a national holiday, to be celebrated by _____
PLURAL NOUN

across America. At the time, Thanksgiving was only celebrated by a few

_____. Sarah wrote _____ letters to one president
PLURAL NOUN   ADJECTIVE

after another, trying to convince them of how _____
ADJECTIVE

Thanksgiving was. No one listened—at least not until President

_____. He/She declared Thanksgiving a/an _____
PERSON IN ROOM   ADJECTIVE

holiday in 1863, and _____ everywhere have been
PLURAL NOUN

celebrating it ever since.

MAD LIBS® is fun to play with friends, but you can also play it by yourself! To begin with, DO NOT look at the story on the page below. Fill in the blanks on this page with the words called for. Then, using the words you have selected, fill in the blank spaces in the story.

Now you've created your own hilarious MAD LIBS® game!

LIFE'S A MAIZE

ADJECTIVE _____

NOUN _____

ADJECTIVE _____

NOUN _____

NOUN _____

VERB ENDING IN "ING" _____

NOUN _____

PLURAL NOUN _____

PLURAL NOUN _____

NOUN _____

PLURAL NOUN _____

PLURAL NOUN _____

ADJECTIVE _____

PLURAL NOUN _____

NOUN _____

NOUN _____

PLURAL NOUN _____

NOUN _____

MAD LIBS®

LIFE'S A MAIZE

Corn is a/an _____ staple of the autumn harvest, and it
            ADJECTIVE

can be found on many a Thanksgiving _____. But corn
                                        NOUN

has many other _____ uses, too! Corn can be found in:
                    ADJECTIVE

Food products: Aside from corn on the _____, you can
                                              NOUN

find corn in _____ butter, _____gum,
                  NOUN   VERB ENDING IN "ING"

and _____ sodas.
        NOUN

Plastics: Plastics made from corn _____ are more
                                          PLURAL NOUN

popular than ever before. You can often recycle plastic

_____ made from corn, too!
    PLURAL NOUN

Fuel: Ethanol is a popular corn _____ used to fuel cars,
                                        NOUN

_____, and even rocket _____.
    PLURAL NOUN   PLURAL NOUN

Household products: Manufacturers often use corn to help make

_____ soaps, scented _____, _____
    ADJECTIVE   PLURAL NOUN   NOUN

polish, and even _____ batteries!
                      NOUN

Everywhere you look, corn _____ can be found. It's not
                              PLURAL NOUN

just a super food, it's a super _____, too!
                                    NOUN

MAD LIBS® is fun to play with friends, but you can also play it by yourself! To begin with, DO NOT look at the story on the page below. Fill in the blanks on this page with the words called for. Then, using the words you have selected, fill in the blank spaces in the story.

Now you've created your own hilarious MAD LIBS® game!

STUFFING YOURSELF SILLY

NOUN _____

NOUN _____

ADJECTIVE _____

PLURAL NOUN _____

PLURAL NOUN _____

PLURAL NOUN _____

NOUN _____

NOUN _____

ADJECTIVE _____

SILLY WORD _____

SAME SILLY WORD _____

PLURAL NOUN _____

PART OF THE BODY _____

PLURAL NOUN _____

NOUN _____

NOUN _____

MAD LIBS®
STUFFING YOURSELF SILLY

Thanksgiving is not a/an _____ to be taken lightly. In order
                              NOUN

to eat as much _____ as possible, you need to have a/an
                      NOUN

_____ strategy. Follow these handy dandy _____ ,
   ADJECTIVE   PLURAL NOUN

and you, too, can own Thanksgiving.

Tip #1: Load up on the most popular _____ first.
                                              PLURAL NOUN

Mashed _____ and gravy tend to be the first to go, and
            PLURAL NOUN

sweet potato _____ and cranberry _____ go
                   NOUN   NOUN

fast, too. Get 'em while they're _____!
                                      ADJECTIVE

Tip #2: Stick with light meat. Dark meat contains more

_____ than light meat, and everyone knows that
   SILLY WORD

_____ makes you sleepy when you eat it. If you're
   SAME SILLY WORD

sleeping, you won't be able to eat _____!
                                        PLURAL NOUN

Tip #3: Don't worry about saving room in your _____
                                                      PART OF THE BODY

for dessert. Studies by famous _____ show that no
                                    PLURAL NOUN

matter how much _____ you've eaten, you always have
                      NOUN

room for dessert—especially if it's _____ pie!
                                          NOUN

MAD LIBS® is fun to play with friends, but you can also play it by yourself! To begin with, DO NOT look at the story on the page below. Fill in the blanks on this page with the words called for. Then, using the words you have selected, fill in the blank spaces in the story.

Now you've created your own hilarious MAD LIBS® game!

CANADIAN THANKSGIVING

NUMBER _____

A PLACE _____

PERSON IN ROOM _____

ADJECTIVE _____

NOUN _____

ADJECTIVE _____

PLURAL NOUN _____

PLURAL NOUN _____

ADJECTIVE _____

MAD LIBS

CANADIAN THANKSGIVING

Did you know that the first Thanksgiving in North America was

actually in Canada, _____ years before the Pilgrims arrived in
                        NUMBER

(the) _____? The first Canadian Thanksgiving took place
        A PLACE

in 1578, when explorer _____ arrived in Newfoundland
                          PERSON IN ROOM

and wanted to give thanks for his/her _____ arrival in the
                                          ADJECTIVE

New World. Beginning in 1957, Canadian Parliament declared that

the second Monday in October would be a day to celebrate "the

bountiful _____ with which Canada has been blessed." Today,
            NOUN

Canadians celebrate their own _____ Thanksgiving, which
                                  ADJECTIVE

is similar to American Thanksgiving in many ways. Canadians eat

turkey and _____, and they watch Canadian football, too!
              PLURAL NOUN

Most importantly, Canadians give thanks for all of their _____.
                                                            PLURAL NOUN

And what's more _____ than that, eh?
                    ADJECTIVE

MAD LIBS® is fun to play with friends, but you can also play it by yourself! To begin with, DO NOT look at the story on the page below. Fill in the blanks on this page with the words called for. Then, using the words you have selected, fill in the blank spaces in the story.

Now you've created your own hilarious MAD LIBS® game!

A THANKSGIVING SPECIAL

A PLACE _____

ADJECTIVE _____

VERB (PAST TENSE) _____

NOUN _____

EXCLAMATION _____

NOUN _____

NOUN _____

ADJECTIVE _____

PERSON IN ROOM (MALE) _____

NOUN _____

ADJECTIVE _____

ADJECTIVE _____

PLURAL NOUN _____

PLURAL NOUN _____

NOUN _____

NOUN _____

NOUN _____

PLURAL NOUN _____

PLURAL NOUN _____

NOUN _____

MAD LIBS®

A THANKSGIVING SPECIAL

It was Thanksgiving, and all the people in (the) _____ were
A PLACE

ready for their annual Thanksgiving celebration. There was just one

problem: The _____ turkey was missing! The townspeople
ADJECTIVE

_____ high and low, but the _____ was nowhere
VERB (PAST TENSE) NOUN

to be found. "_____!" little Sally _____ said. "We can't
EXCLAMATION NOUN

have Thanksgiving without a/an _____!" Just then, a/an
NOUN

_____ figure appeared. It was _____, the
ADJECTIVE PERSON IN ROOM (MALE)

mean old _____ who lived on top of a/an _____ hill and
NOUN ADJECTIVE

never came to visit. "I took your _____ turkey!" he shouted.
ADJECTIVE

"You _____ are so thankful, but what do you have to be
PLURAL NOUN

thankful for?" "We have our friends, our families, and our

_____!" said little Sally _____. "Just because *you*
PLURAL NOUN NOUN

don't have any doesn't mean you should ruin our Thanksgiving, you

mean old _____!" The townspeople cheered, and the grumpy
NOUN

_____ saw the error of his ways. He returned the town turkey
NOUN

and joined the _____ in celebration. "Happy Thanksgiving
PLURAL NOUN

to _____ everywhere!" little Sally _____ cheered.
PLURAL NOUN NOUN

MAD LIBS® is fun to play with friends, but you can also play it by yourself! To begin with, DO NOT look at the story on the page below. Fill in the blanks on this page with the words called for. Then, using the words you have selected, fill in the blank spaces in the story.

Now you've created your own hilarious MAD LIBS® game!

PILGRIM KID

ADJECTIVE _____

PLURAL NOUN _____

NOUN _____

PART OF THE BODY _____

PLURAL NOUN _____

NOUN _____

NOUN _____

PERSON IN ROOM (MALE) _____

PERSON IN ROOM (FEMALE) _____

ADJECTIVE _____

ADJECTIVE _____

ADVERB _____

PART OF THE BODY (PLURAL) _____

NOUN _____

VERB (PAST TENSE) _____

MAD LIBS

PILGRIM KID

Dear Ye Olde Diary,

Life as a wee Pilgrim child is more _____ by the day. Today,
                                      ADJECTIVE

Mother sent me to the garden to pick some fresh _____
                                                  PLURAL NOUN

for supper. The sun was hot, and I was wearing my black-and-white

_____, which did not keep my _____ cool.
     NOUN   PART OF THE BODY

Afterward, Father insisted I help him hunt for _____ using
                                                 PLURAL NOUN

a bow and _____, but we only shot one small _____.
               NOUN   NOUN

Alas! While Mother and Father cooked dinner, I went to play with my

brother _____ and sister _____,
          PERSON IN ROOM (MALE)   PERSON IN ROOM (FEMALE)

but we hath only one toy—a/an _____ rock. Our _____
                                ADJECTIVE   ADJECTIVE

game of Kick the Rock soon became _____ tiresome. Nay, we
                                      ADVERB

were bored out of our _____! Aye, life as a Pilgrim
                       PART OF THE BODY (PLURAL)

_____ is not all it's _____ up to be!
    NOUN   VERB (PAST TENSE)

MAD LIBS® is fun to play with friends, but you can also play it by yourself! To begin with, DO NOT look at the story on the page below. Fill in the blanks on this page with the words called for. Then, using the words you have selected, fill in the blank spaces in the story.

Now you've created your own hilarious MAD LIBS® game!

THE LAST TURKEY

NOUN _____

A PLACE _____

ADJECTIVE _____

TYPE OF ANIMAL _____

ADJECTIVE _____

PERSON IN ROOM _____

NOUN _____

PART OF THE BODY (PLURAL) _____

PLURAL NOUN _____

PLURAL NOUN _____

VERB ENDING IN "ING" _____

VERB ENDING IN "ING" _____

SAME VERB ENDING IN "ING" _____

PERSON IN ROOM (FEMALE) _____

ADJECTIVE _____

ADJECTIVE _____

ADJECTIVE _____

THE LAST TURKEY

It was Thanksgiving, and our family didn't have a/an _____ to
NOUN

roast. We hopped in the car and drove to (the) _____, but
A PLACE

they were all out of _____ turkeys. "We have ham and duck
ADJECTIVE

and _____, though!" said the man at the deli counter.
TYPE OF ANIMAL

"It's not Thanksgiving without a/an _____ turkey!" my dad
ADJECTIVE

replied. So we got back in the car and drove to _____'s
PERSON IN ROOM

Grocery. They had one turkey left—but another _____
NOUN

grabbed the turkey before we could get our _____
PART OF THE BODY (PLURAL)

on it. "Come on, _____," said my mom. "Let's just go
PLURAL NOUN

out for Chinese _____ instead." But on the drive to the
PLURAL NOUN

restaurant, we spotted a wild turkey _____ across the
VERB ENDING IN "ING"

road. "Are you _____ what I'm _____?"
VERB ENDING IN "ING"   SAME VERB ENDING IN "ING"

my sister _____ said. We all got out of the car
PERSON IN ROOM (FEMALE)

and chased the _____ bird down the road. But once we got
ADJECTIVE

the _____ turkey home, we couldn't bear to eat him—so we
ADJECTIVE

made him our _____ family pet instead!
ADJECTIVE

From GOBBLE GOBBLE MAD LIBS® • Copyright © 2013 by Penguin Random House LLC.

MAD LIBS® is fun to play with friends, but you can also play it by yourself! To begin with, DO NOT look at the story on the page below. Fill in the blanks on this page with the words called for. Then, using the words you have selected, fill in the blank spaces in the story.

Now you've created your own hilarious MAD LIBS® game!

THANKS, SQUANTO

NOUN _____

A PLACE _____

VERB (PAST TENSE) _____

VERB (PAST TENSE) _____

ADJECTIVE _____

ADJECTIVE _____

VERB _____

PLURAL NOUN _____

PLURAL NOUN _____

PLURAL NOUN _____

ADJECTIVE _____

ADJECTIVE _____

The first Thanksgiving would never have been possible without

Squanto, a Native American _____. Squanto had learned to speak
                              NOUN

English in (the) _____, England. When Squanto left England
                  A PLACE

and _____ back to America, he discovered that his
     VERB (PAST TENSE)

tribe no longer _____ there. In 1620, Squanto settled
                 VERB (PAST TENSE)

with the _____ Pilgrims, who had just survived a/an
          ADJECTIVE

_____ winter. The Pilgrims, it turned out, had no idea how to
 ADJECTIVE

_____ in the New World. Luckily, Squanto taught them how
 VERB

to plant _____, fish for _____, and hunt for
          PLURAL NOUN   PLURAL NOUN

wild _____. Without Squanto's help, the Pilgrims would
      PLURAL NOUN

never have survived, much less had food to make a/an _____
                                                      ADJECTIVE

feast for the first Thanksgiving. Maybe this Thanksgiving we should

give thanks for Squanto. After all, if it weren't for him, we wouldn't

celebrate this _____ holiday!
                ADJECTIVE

MAD LIBS® is fun to play with friends, but you can also play it by yourself! To begin with, DO NOT look at the story on the page below. Fill in the blanks on this page with the words called for. Then, using the words you have selected, fill in the blank spaces in the story.

Now you've created your own hilarious MAD LIBS® game!

THANKSGIVING FACTS

PLURAL NOUN _____

PLURAL NOUN _____

NUMBER _____

ADJECTIVE _____

NOUN _____

NOUN _____

NOUN _____

PLURAL NOUN _____

PLURAL NOUN _____

PLURAL NOUN _____

PLURAL NOUN _____

PLURAL NOUN _____

VERB (PAST TENSE) _____

PLURAL NOUN _____

PLURAL NOUN _____

MAD LIBS
THANKSGIVING FACTS

- Each Thanksgiving, _____ in the United States
  _{PLURAL NOUN}

consume forty-six million _____. That's almost _____
  _{PLURAL NOUN}   _{NUMBER}

pounds of turkey per person!

- _____ inventor and politician Benjamin Franklin wanted
  _{ADJECTIVE}

the turkey to be the national _____ of the United States.
  _{NOUN}

- TV dinners originated when a company called _____
  _{NOUN}

had too much leftover frozen _____ after Thanksgiving;
  _{NOUN}

they began packaging the turkey with potatoes, _____,
  _{PLURAL NOUN}

and other foods into the first frozen meals.

- The tradition of Thanksgiving football began when the owner of

the Detroit _____ wanted to build up the team's
  _{PLURAL NOUN}

loyal _____. On Thanksgiving Day 1934, they
  _{PLURAL NOUN}

played the Chicago _____ and lost.
  _{PLURAL NOUN}

- According to *Guinness World* _____, the largest
  _{PLURAL NOUN}

pumpkin pie ever _____ weighed two thousand
  _{VERB (PAST TENSE)}

_____ and was over twelve _____ long.
  _{PLURAL NOUN}   _{PLURAL NOUN}

MAD LIBS® is fun to play with friends, but you can also play it by yourself! To begin with, DO NOT look at the story on the page below. Fill in the blanks on this page with the words called for. Then, using the words you have selected, fill in the blank spaces in the story.

Now you've created your own hilarious MAD LIBS® game!

PARDON THAT TURKEY

PLURAL NOUN _____

ADJECTIVE _____

PLURAL NOUN _____

ADJECTIVE _____

NOUN _____

COLOR _____

PLURAL NOUN _____

A PLACE _____

ADJECTIVE _____

VERB _____

ADJECTIVE _____

PERSON IN ROOM _____

ADJECTIVE _____

ADJECTIVE _____

VERB (PAST TENSE) _____

MAD LIBS

PARDON THAT TURKEY

Each year, the president of the United _____ is presented
                                        PLURAL NOUN

with two _____ turkeys to pardon. That means he spares them
         ADJECTIVE

from being eaten by _____ on Thanksgiving. The president
                    PLURAL NOUN

formally pardons the _____ birds in the _____
                      ADJECTIVE   NOUN

Garden of the _____ House, while television _____
               COLOR   PLURAL NOUN

and families from all over (the) _____ witness the
                                  A PLACE

_____ spectacle. The pardoned turkeys get to _____
ADJECTIVE   VERB

out the rest of their days on a/an _____ farm at President
                                    ADJECTIVE

_____'s estate, Mount Vernon. To this day, twenty-two
PERSON IN ROOM

_____ turkeys have been pardoned by the _____
ADJECTIVE   ADJECTIVE

president. To those turkeys, it must feel like they've _____
                                                       VERB (PAST TENSE)

the lottery!

MAD LIBS® is fun to play with friends, but you can also play it by yourself! To begin with, DO NOT look at the story on the page below. Fill in the blanks on this page with the words called for. Then, using the words you have selected, fill in the blank spaces in the story.

Now you've created your own hilarious MAD LIBS® game!

PICK YOUR PIE

VERB ENDING IN "ING" _____

NOUN _____

ADJECTIVE _____

ADJECTIVE _____

PLURAL NOUN _____

ADJECTIVE _____

ADJECTIVE _____

VERB _____

ADJECTIVE _____

ADJECTIVE _____

ADJECTIVE _____

NOUN _____

ADJECTIVE _____

NOUN _____

MAD LIBS®
PICK YOUR PIE

Do you love _____ pie on Thanksgiving? Who doesn't!

VERB ENDING IN "ING"

The only problem is choosing which _____ to eat! Take this

NOUN

quiz to find out your _____ preference!

ADJECTIVE

1. Your favorite kind of pie involves (a) _____ slices of

ADJECTIVE

   fruit, (b) nuts and _____, (c) _____ vegetables.

PLURAL NOUN ADJECTIVE

2. Of these three _____ options, your favorite color of food

ADJECTIVE

   to _____ is (a) yellow, (b) brown, or (c) orange.

VERB

3. Do you prefer your food to be (a) gooey and sweet with a touch

   of _____ cinnamon, (b) sweet with a sprinkling of

ADJECTIVE

   _____ salt, or (c) mushy and _____.

ADJECTIVE ADJECTIVE

If you picked mostly *a*'s, apple _____ is your favorite

NOUN

Thanksgiving treat. If you picked mostly *b*'s, you are a fan of

_____ pecan pie. If you picked mostly *c*'s, you can't say

ADJECTIVE

no to a heaping _____ of pumpkin or sweet potato pie!

NOUN

MAD LIBS® is fun to play with friends, but you can also play it by yourself! To begin with, DO NOT look at the story on the page below. Fill in the blanks on this page with the words called for. Then, using the words you have selected, fill in the blank spaces in the story.

Now you've created your own hilarious MAD LIBS® game!

EXCERPT FROM A THANKSGIVING PAGEANT

ADJECTIVE _____

NOUN _____

ADJECTIVE _____

PLURAL NOUN _____

PLURAL NOUN _____

ADJECTIVE _____

PLURAL NOUN _____

NOUN _____

ADJECTIVE _____

ADJECTIVE _____

PLURAL NOUN _____

ADJECTIVE _____

EXCLAMATION _____

NOUN _____

ADJECTIVE _____

MAD LIBS®
EXCERPT FROM A
THANKSGIVING PAGEANT

This is a/an _____ scene from a children's Thanksgiving
          ADJECTIVE

_____ pageant. This scene can be read aloud by several
   NOUN

_____ _____.
   ADJECTIVE   PLURAL NOUN

Pilgrim #1: Welcome to the first Thanksgiving, our dear friends

and _____!
        PLURAL NOUN

Pilgrim #2: We want to say a/an _____ thank-you to
                                    ADJECTIVE

our Native American _____, without whom this
                          PLURAL NOUN

_____ would not be possible!
   NOUN

Native American #1: Thank you, _____ Pilgrims! We
                                        ADJECTIVE

appreciate your sharing this _____ harvest with us.
                                  ADJECTIVE

Native American #2: Yes, we can't wait to eat these tasty

_____! We are thankful for your _____
   PLURAL NOUN   ADJECTIVE

friendship.

Pilgrim #1: _____! Let's eat this _____ before
                   EXCLAMATION   NOUN

it gets _____!
            ADJECTIVE

MAD LIBS® is fun to play with friends, but you can also play it by yourself! To begin with, DO NOT look at the story on the page below. Fill in the blanks on this page with the words called for. Then, using the words you have selected, fill in the blank spaces in the story.

Now you've created your own hilarious MAD LIBS® game!

WHAT IN THE GOURD?

PLURAL NOUN _____

PLURAL NOUN _____

ADJECTIVE _____

PLURAL NOUN _____

PLURAL NOUN _____

ADJECTIVE _____

ADJECTIVE _____

ADJECTIVE _____

PLURAL NOUN _____

TYPE OF LIQUID _____

PLURAL NOUN _____

PLURAL NOUN _____

PLURAL NOUN _____

VERB _____

NOUN _____

MAD LIBS
WHAT IN THE GOURD?

Gourds are funny little _____ often used to decorate
                              PLURAL NOUN

holiday _____ at Thanksgiving. But what *are* these
          PLURAL NOUN

_____ little _____? They may look like tiny
  ADJECTIVE   PLURAL NOUN

pumpkins or miniature _____, but you don't want to eat
                          PLURAL NOUN

them. They smell _____ and they taste _____, too.
                    ADJECTIVE   ADJECTIVE

Gourds are related to squash and pumpkins, and they are considered

a/an _____ fruit. But unlike those _____, they
        ADJECTIVE   PLURAL NOUN

are used only for decoration or to store _____ or other
                                          TYPE OF LIQUID

_____. They are also often used as musical _____.
  PLURAL NOUN   PLURAL NOUN

Gourds are adorable little _____, but look, don't
                             PLURAL NOUN

_____, when you see them on your Thanksgiving
    VERB

_____!
   NOUN

MAD LIBS® is fun to play with friends, but you can also play it by yourself! To begin with, DO NOT look at the story on the page below. Fill in the blanks on this page with the words called for. Then, using the words you have selected, fill in the blank spaces in the story.

Now you've created your own hilarious MAD LIBS® game!

TOM THE TURKEY

PLURAL NOUN _____

NOUN _____

PLURAL NOUN _____

NOUN _____

NOUN _____

PART OF THE BODY _____

NOUN _____

NOUN _____

PLURAL NOUN _____

NOUN _____

PLURAL NOUN _____

NOUN _____

PLURAL NOUN _____

ADJECTIVE _____

NOUN _____

NOUN _____

TOM THE TURKEY

On Christmas, _____ get visited by Santa Claus. On Easter,
          PLURAL NOUN

the Easter Bunny hops into your _____. But who comes to give
                                      NOUN

you _____ on Thanksgiving? Tom the Turkey, that's who!
        PLURAL NOUN

If you have been a thankful little girl or _____, Tom the Turkey
                                                NOUN

just might come visit your _____ on Thanksgiving. While you
                                  NOUN

rest your pretty little _____ during your post-meal nap,
                         PART OF THE BODY

this magical _____ flies through the _____ and leaves
                  NOUN   NOUN

cornucopias filled with _____ at your front _____.
                            PLURAL NOUN   NOUN

Your cornucopia might be filled with candy, presents, and

_____, if you're lucky. But if you've been an ungrateful
    PLURAL NOUN

little _____, you'll get a cornucopia filled with _____!
          NOUN   PLURAL NOUN

So be a/an _____ little _____, and maybe this year
            ADJECTIVE   NOUN

Tom the Turkey will come to your _____!
                                      NOUN